Verseology

The therapy of creating
Song and verse

By

Graham Huff

Verseology

The therapy of creating Song and verse

1ˢᵗ Edition

ISBN: 978-0-9561515-1-3

ISBN 978-0-9561515-1-3

9 780956 151513   90000 >

Verseology

The therapy of creating Song and verse

Contents

Forward – what is *Verseology*

The practice of Verseology is the process of coming to terms with deeply held feelings and emotions, and channelling these and other senses into song, verse and poetry. The practice of Verseology can be thinking about anything that causes an emotional response in you; it can be about love and happiness, or any of life's experiences that give you pleasure; but where Verseology is at its most powerful is when we are haunted by that skeleton in the cupboard: the demon who slowly emerges out of the dark and foggy background of the mind.

In confronting these feelings in an honest, sincere and rational way we can 'come to terms' with these 'skeletons in the cupboard' or 'demons' as I like to call them; they lay deep in the depths of our subconscious mind, laying dormant until an event that troubles us causes our defences to weaken and then they come to the foreground of our minds, trying to bring chaos and doubt to our everyday lives. Some of us already have ways of dealing with these events, but some of us don't and can spend a lifetime suffering the emotional turmoil and havoc that these demons can inflict. In my own case I was in my early 50's before I accidentally came across a way of effectively dealing with these demons, this is how it happened:

I decided in 2003 that I would like to learn to play the guitar, and decided to purchase a second hand instrument that was in good working order, but cheap. Along with my book of guitar chords I practiced every day and soon became reasonably competent at playing the instrument. From this point I branched out into the world of songwriting, learning from various books and from a wealth of information on the internet.

I wrote my first song in the autumn of 2003 and chose a subject that was not only close to my heart: it was a skeleton in the cupboard, or rather, a demon lurking somewhere in the back of my mind that would try to 'come out' on occasions. This would cause me a certain amount of anxiety and low mood, the sort of thing that gets you down for a couple of hours until you are able to overcome it, and get on with your life.

I decided whilst writing the lyrics of this song that total honesty on my part was a must; the resulting few days turned out to be very addictive, I just could not put my pen down, I became engulfed with this process of thinking about and analyzing my emotions and feelings; I just had to carry on until the song was finished.

With the song finished and simply recorded into a Dictaphone, I realized what an emotional roller coaster that I had been on; yes, I had experienced goose bumps and even a few tears on some occasions , but now that the song was written, I felt elation, and a sense of real achievement that I had beaten this particular demon; almost a form of self exorcism; *a self help therapy.*

I still find now, some five years on, that when I play this song I still get immense satisfaction from listening to it; along with the occasional goose bump. If the demon starts to creep forward into my conscious mind, then I will play my song or recite my verse: This brings back into my mind the process that I originally went through in coming to terms with this demon, and brings back my confidence and fortitude in knowing that I have tamed this demon once, and can do so once again. This is what I call the practice of *Verseology*. It is *not* something that I just dreamed up, it is a powerful experience that actually happened to me.

When our self help therapy is used to overcome a

skeleton in the cupboard, there are two distinctive approaches that I have found to be very effective, these are:

1.   **Confront the subject head-on;** take it on in a fair, honest and above all rational way; be the judge and jury. Accept what has happened and take some time to really understand what did actually happen. Ask the questions, was anyone at fault, were your actions and attitude fair and reasonable, and apply some lateral thinking; what could have been the motives or feelings towards what happened: maybe when you view the situation from other viewpoints, then what came to pass was only fair after all. The main point here is to take your time and consider all viewpoints with genuine fairness, but above all, be completely honest with yourself. Try to reach a point of closure, you have been the subject, judge and jury in this exercise. Hopefully you have come to some sort of conclusion that you think is fair and reasonable, even if you accept that you yourself should carry some or all of the blame.

Remember, you don't have to disclose any of your thoughts to anyone else, they are private and personal to you. If you want to keep your song, verse or poem a secret and only use it when you want to, that's fine. On the other hand you might want to share your work with a close friend or even an adversary, as a way of making up: think carefully before taking any action, but in my own experience sharing some of your personal thoughts can really reinforce what you have already achieved.

2.   **Take avoiding action.** You may feel that this particular skeleton in the cupboard is best avoided, at least for the time being. Now is the time to find a theme or subject that evokes a strong emotion in you, the stronger the better. Every time that the demon starts to creep into your mind, you will use this subject to distract your thoughts away from the demon; rather like the practice of repeating a mantra, only in your case you will be using your song or verse. Be patient and repeat this strategy as often as you have to; you will be surprised at how quickly the mind learns this process and almost does it automatically.

Now that we have an idea of what Verseology is all about, we really do have a starting point. You will have experienced a lot of emotions and experiences in your life, and now is the time to pick on a subject that you want to take to task. Take it on in a fair and honest way by going through the various sections of this book and analyse what happened; you might even shed a few tears on your journey: well, that is all part of the process of Verseology.

The following pages are taken and adapted from my book entitled Songwriting for Beginners. The method and the process is exactly the same for Verseology, as I tend to write my songs and verse from the heart anyway, but just to make sure that you don't loose your focus, I would suggest that every now and again you re-read the Forward – What is Verseology, just as a reminder.

Good luck on your journey and please feel free to visit my web site at www.verseology.co.uk where you can participate by uploading your work, or join the forum and talk to like minded people, including myself
'Bon voyage'

Introduction

I have loved listening to music all of my life, yet had never tried to learn to play a musical instrument. I was suddenly inspired some years ago whilst watching a musical TV reality show that, on one occasion, required the participating students to compose a song. There followed, over a number of days a fascinating insight into song writing, with a number of successful commercial songwriters acting as both tutors and mentors to the students. Lyrics and poetry were created, song structure and form were explained, simple musical arrangements on a guitar were made and suddenly, to my astonishment, some very credible sounding songs started to emerge, I was hooked.

No single aspect or individual task of writing these songs seemed to me to be very difficult to achieve on their own, but when moulded and fused together in the right order, they sounded great.

I decided that I would 'have a go' at writing a song for myself. It took only a few minutes of thinking about the subject of my song for me to realise that there were many, many things that had happened in my life that I just had to write about. They say that there's a book waiting to be written in everyone, I say that there's also a song waiting to be composed.

So started my life's journey to becoming a self taught songwriter and musician. You will not realise at this point in time, especially if this is the start of your song writing journey, the sheer amount of pleasure and self satisfaction that you will get from writing your own song or verse and listening to it on your tape or CD player. It is not only totally addictive, it is also a very therapeutic process that you go through, especially if you write about emotional or sentimental experiences that have happened in your life. It still makes the goose pimples stand up on my arms and neck when I play some of my very simple and basic songs from when I started song writing.

Another point to note of going through this process, is that you can keep your song or lyrics as a secret known only to you. On the other hand you might want to play it to a friend or loved one, or you might want the whole world to hear your song and put it up onto the internet, the choice is yours.

Please believe me when I say that there's nothing hard about writing song and verse. Follow the process and techniques that you will learn from this book, and the song will come together much more easily than you think.

I have included a basic introduction to the guitar and I would urge you to have a go at learning to play the instrument. Buy a cheap second hand instrument to start, or borrow from a friend, but please just give it a try. It only takes three chords to write the music for a basic song. If you decide that playing an instrument is just not for you then don't fret, you can still write the lyrics and vocal melody which can be just as meaningful in their own right.

Finally, let me also assure you that you do not need to know lots of music theory to write and compose the music for a simple song. So many people have told me about music teachers who display a certain amount of arrogance when it comes to learning music theory and a musical instrument, expecting the student to learn unnecessarily difficult theory and chords. This book tells you what you need to know, simply, to write your first song or verse and hopefully play your first musical chords.

Some publications that teach song writing tend to try and inspire the reader by making lists of your favourite songs, usually comprising of classic songs from very talented and famous artists and then carrying out various analyses of the songs, including likes and dislikes. This is all well and good and I would certainly recommend spending as much time as you can listening to and analysing songs, but there is a trap that you can fall into if you are not aware of it:

1. You are being taken along a road of very high expectations. At this stage it's very easy to get frustrated because you can't find that wonderful lyric full of meaning and emotion.

2. At this stage don't expect too much of yourself, aim for simple but meaningful lyrics, the more sophisticated lyrics will come with practice and as you grow in confidence and experience.

There are a number of ways that a song can be written, for example, shall I start with the lyrics, or the melody, or a chord progression. This book is biased towards writing the lyrics first and it's this way because that's the way that I usually write my own songs, a personal preference. Having said that, I have written a couple of songs starting off with the chord progression and rhythm. You can of course change the order of the lessons as you work through the book to suit your own style, but I would recommend that you write your first song following the lesson order in the book.

I tend to write songs that are based on my personal experiences and observations of life, so for me it's a natural starting point. You will develop your own preferences as well as your own style as your list of song titles grow.

This book assumes no previous knowledge of song writing, musical theory, or that you can play a musical instrument. It is the aim of this book to guide you through the very same process of learning that I went through myself: what you need to provide is lots of enthusiasm and time to think and practice.

The rules and goals of song writing

There are many rules in the world of music theory and composition, but in my opinion, they are all there to be broken.

If every songwriter followed the rules to the letter then we would soon have songs being produced that all sounded similar, and no new genres would emerge.

The rules that govern musical keys and chords are important and should always be in the back of your mind when composing, but use your ears and instinct first. These rules are explained in this book in a simple enough manner. Trust in yourself and in your ears. If it sounds good to you, then that's the most important thing because you are the artist, expressing yourself in your way. Don't be swayed by friends or peer pressure, be yourself and stand by your work. Of course, it's always good to have genuine critique of your work for you to consider. This will vary between those who like your work, those who don't and those in between. If your future song writing aspirations are to get a top ten chart hit with the bands and singers that are 'in vogue' at the time, then you will of course have to follow and copy their styles and techniques.

There is however one rule that I never break when song writing, that is:

1st *rule of song writing*

Lay yourself naked and bare your soul to the world.

That does not mean of course that you have to run around naked. This could mean expressing and talking about deep emotion and feelings, or it could be about singing the joys and happiness of life and loved ones. There are of course endless categories in between and either side, but it must be a true and honest emotion or feeling.

There are some songwriters and artists who take issue with this rule and say that you should not go too far when writing about your personal emotion and feelings. A good example of this is the 1970 album 'Blue' by 'Joni Mitchell'. Some of the songs are so full of emotion that if I'm in the right mood and setting when listening, I get taken away to somewhere else for a few minutes and my whole mood is changed.

That for me is what song writing is all about, transporting the listener to another place where you can sense and feel the emotion that the songwriter put into the song. Many people will also relate the lyrics to themselves and their own experiences. For your song to be successful, you should try to: *Make the listener believe your lyrics*

All of the great classic songs allow the listener to relate to the lyrics, because they have probably experienced the emotions expressed in the song themselves. When others ask me about writing good songs, I always answer simply by saying, touch the listener's emotions, give them goose pimples or make the hairs on the back of their neck stand up.

2nd rule of songwriting:

Touch the listener's emotions

Take some time now to consider these 2 rules. They are both complimentary to one another, and both need each other. I don't think that one will work without the other: honesty from the heart will always be believed.

3rd rule of songwriting:

Add some degree of structure

This will be fully explained in the section on song structure, but for now, listen to one or two of your favourite songs and listen for the sections of the song that are repeated.

It is this repetition of the music and lyrics that we learn quite quickly that gets locked into our memory. It's the parts of the song that you whistle or sing to yourself that are important to the songwriter; these are often referred to as hooks.

Key point

A musical hook is a part, or parts of a song that stick in the memory. The part that you tend to hum, whistle or even sing. It may be a catchy one line lyric or it may be a short guitar riff for example.

Tools of the trade

I would recommend that you acquire the following items for your songwriting:

Good quality dictionary – make sure that the meaning of the words fit the sentiment.

Thesaurus – Can give you fresh ideas when checking the meaning of a word.

Rhyming dictionary – Can help you find the missing word that rhymes with the previous lines.

Hardback workbook – Keep a record of everything, including date entry for all of your work. Never throw anything away.

Hardback songbook – Write your lyrics and chords used out in full along with a description of the story line and explain your sentiments.

Pocket recorder – Digital recorder or mobile phone. This is essential when you are working on vocal melodies. Just hum the tune or sing into the recorder. If you don't record it straight away you will forget it and loose it.

Storyline, lyrics and subject matter.

The beauty of songwriting from a creative

viewpoint is that the songs lyrics can tell a story about anything. You don't necessarily need a complete story with beginning, middle and end. You could for example just take out a section from the middle of the story that holds a particular interest for you. It does not need a reason, and it does not need to come to a conclusion: you can leave the listener to draw their own conclusions if they want to. It also does not need to be a story, you can write about feelings and emotions, the animal world, politics or injustices, the list is endless, but wonderfully, the choice is yours.

Also consider at this point the emotion that you are trying to sing about and your intended audience (if there is one), this could mean:

Joy & happiness – great to dance to

So sad it makes me want to cry

That gave me goose pimples

I love you so much – embracing / dancing

I hate you so much – why did you do it

The list is endless

Take some time now to think of some more story lines, feelings and emotions and write them down in your workbook. Consider the personal experiences that have happened in your life, both good and bad.
Indulge yourself in fantasy, sometimes take the story past your own experiences. Fantasize the situation to new highs and lows, revel in your dreams and let your mind drift and experience the emotions of these fantasies.

Some songwriters use their own personal experiences and demons to write about. The first rule of songwriting applies here, because if you are not totally honest with yourself and you don't write about your true feelings and emotions, the listener will quickly decide that your lyric is not true or plausible and probably won't want to listen to your song again. On the other hand if the listener believes in what you are saying, then there's a good chance that you will fulfil the second rule of songwriting and touch the emotion of the listener, as a songwriter you have just scored a goal and achieved what you set out to do.

Key point

It's only when you have been through this process that you find the first hidden benefit of songwriting, it can be very therapeutic for you. The process of writing about and examining all of the emotions held in your mind about past experiences, are by some mechanism released, freeing or releasing these emotions or in some cases, exorcising the demons. Of course these emotions can also be happy joyful memories like when you first fell in love or the birth of a child.

Getting the story down on paper

Now that you have got the outline of the story or theme, it's time to start analysing it and writing it all down on paper. Write down as many one off sentences that you can about all aspects of your songs subject. Try to find some quiet time for yourself and start to focus your thoughts on your subject. Try to go into a 'day dream' sort of state and visualise your story, bring back memories into the mind and if possible, relive your experiences. Sometimes songs and lyrics almost write themselves when you have gotten yourself into the right frame of mind, just flowing from your pen, faster than you can write. On other occasions you may need to map out your story and fill in the various parts as you work on the various themes of your story. If some thoughts seem to have come to a dead end, then just move on for now and write about what does come into your head: *just keep writing*.

Sentences don't have to flow into one another at this stage, just try to get all of your thoughts, feelings and emotions onto paper.

Warning – You may find yourself waking up in the middle of the night with a great idea or line of verse, so make sure that you put a notebook and pen by your bedside. That way you don't loose the line or have to get out of bed. Believe me, when you are in the creative zone, it really does happen.

Forming the storyline

When you have reached the stage where you think that most of your thoughts and feelings about the story are written down on paper, it's time to let it rest for a while.

Your enthusiasm may be such that you can't leave it alone and just want to get on with it, well that's fine if it's the way that you want to work. I like to leave it completely for a day or two and get the story completely out of my mind so that I can return to the storyline sentences and review and maybe add to what I've already written.

Hint

It can be very useful to have 2 or 3 songs and ideas on the go at any one time, as this allows you to switch off from your current song and turn your attention to something else. The biggest benefit here is that you can clear your mind of that song and return to it at a later date with an open mind, thus allowing you to reappraise and review your song content. You may want to add a new dimension or intensify a particular theme, that's fine, just go through the routine again.

Don't be too eager to draw to a close, be patient, and be sure that your content includes everything and more that you want to say on the subject, you can always leave things out of your final draft. You may also find that some lines stand out, having some sort of special meaning; these lines should be developed further.

You may also find that the line hints at being a metaphor.

By definition – a metaphor is a figure of speech in which a word or phrase is applied to an object or action that it does not literally denote in order to imply a resemblance, for example *he is a lion in battle,* or *you are the wind beneath my wings.* Many songs use metaphors to great effect; they can really indulge the listeners thoughts and connect with the emotions.

When you return to your written thoughts, read through all of them several times and you will find that a certain theme or aspect of the story starts to emerge. If you started off with a strong theme in mind, say a love story about a loved one, then you may find some interesting or fascinating details emerge that you didn't realise were part of your feelings and emotions.

Start to focus on the theme that is emerging and put some boundaries on it. You may want to include all of your thoughts that you have written down, or you may want to concentrate on only a certain part or parts.

Decide how the story will start and what sentences to use. What's in the middle and how the story will end, if indeed it does end. Highlight or circle with a pen the sentences and words that form these parts and rewrite them out in a rough order of beginning, middle and end.

Song structure

In general terms, the component parts of a song are:

(A) Verse – this usually changes as the song progresses and tells the story of the song from beginning to end. Most modern songs have 2, 3 or 4 verses and sometimes start off with a double verse.

(B) Chorus – The chorus is usually repeated 2 or 3 times and conveys the main theme or message of the song.

(C) Bridge – A way of linking the verse to the chorus.

The Bridge - My interpretation of a bridge is a few bars of lyrics or rhythm that link 2 passages together, usually the verse with the chorus. This link is usually a musical one where the melodies of the verse and chorus are quite different, but it can also be used to make a short, stark kind of statement that can really kick the chorus into action. See the section 'do I need a bridge' for a more detailed discussion on this subject.

The bridge can raise or lower the tempo, it can change the mood, basically it allows a smooth transition from one section to another. Not all songs use a bridge, some songs are similar enough in verse and chorus to flow naturally from one to the other.

The middle eight

This is an optional section of the song that literally consists of 8 bars, usually from a lead guitar or solo keyboard, placed in the middle of the song. This could be a hooky solo performance that shows off musicianship, or it could be used to break up a song where maybe there isn't enough variation and contrast.

Lyrics, flow and rhyme

Types of rhyme

From your sentences, list the key words that you have used to give the line meaning and impact. Now is the time to think about adding some rhyme and flow to these sentences to further enhance the beauty or dynamic of what you are trying to say. The most widely used types of rhyme are:

Perfect rhyme

The sounds are exactly alike, as in *stone & bone,* and *day & play.*

Imperfect rhyme

This form of rhyme pairs words together that have similar sounds such as *time & mine* and *down & around.*

Open rhyme

This form of rhyme usually ends gently as in *tow & flow* and *sky & pie.*

Inner rhyme

The wall is tall and close to the mall is an example of multiple rhyming within a single sentence.

Free form

This is really the same as free form poetry, it does not have any rules and is a mix of any, or all of the above. It may indeed not contain any rhyme at all, relying on a flow of words that have a distinctive meaning.

Rhyming schemes and the 4 bar section

The 4 bar section is a block of four lines of lyrics that will fit into 4 bars of music in the song. The 4 bars of music do not need to exist at this time. The 4 bar section is the fundamental building block of the whole song and will form all of the verses and the chorus. If four lines of verse is not enough to get your message across, then just double up and use two 4 bar sections, joined together to form an 8 bar section.

Rhyme schemes

Rhyming schemes are numerous and varied, the

important rule here is consistency and repetition. Ideally, the rhyme scheme should establish a pattern of rhyme that is applied to the 4 bar section, and is repeated throughout the song. The most commonly used rhyme schemes are AABB, ABCB and ABAB, but almost any combination is acceptable if it sounds good.

Example – in this example, the rhyming lines are coded with the same letters.

A

A

B

B

In this example, the first two lines rhyme together, and the second two lines rhyme together, so you should also apply this pattern to the next verse, and so on. This gives the song consistency and makes it comfortable to the ear and tends to stick in the memory. Remember that the rhyming scheme for the verse and the chorus will probably be different, so stick to their respective patterns throughout the song.

Other well used rhyming patterns include ABBC, AAAA and AAB/BA where the B/B indicates an internal rhyme in the same line.

As a recurring theme, these rules are again there to be broken. The meaning and the flow of words are sometimes more important than incorporating rhyme just for the sake of making the lines rhyme nicely together.

You may also have a very hooky and rhythmic melody that deserves most of the attention, relegating the lyrics into second place.

Hint

The flow of the lyrics are just as important as the rhyme. Some lyrics don't contain words that rhyme but the lines of verse have a smooth, natural flow when spoken or sung. Often the meaning and emotion of a set of sentences is also more important than rhyme. Just try to find a balance here that simply sounds good, it will come naturally with practice and experience. From your collection of sentences:

List words associated with the subject

List your key words (not the filler words that just make

up the sentence).

Can you make two lines rhyme together, maybe by changing one or two words

Can you change a key word to make two lines rhyme whilst retaining the meaning.

This is the time to pick up your thesaurus and rhyming dictionary and start to practice this word and sentence manipulation.

Verse and Chorus structure

4 bar structure (think of it as 4 lines of verse that have some sort of rhyme).
8 bar structure (this is really two sets of 4 bar that flow nicely together).
This is the essence of your song, a collection of 4 and 8 bar structures that are used by the verse and chorus. A bridge can be two bars or more.
In the example song, Beyond Love, from appendix B,

note and examine the way that I have used 8 bar structures for the verse and 4 bar structures for the chorus.

Start putting lines into 4 bar and 8 bar structures. Can you link together any 4 bar structures into 8 bar ones. You should put together as many 4 and 8 bar structures as you can from the lines in your song. You may need to change the line order, but play around and manipulate your lines of verse and words, changing words where necessary, but still retaining your meaning. This is a process that may seem strange at first, but with the aid of your various books you will be surprised how, with a little time and effort you are able to shape these sentences into verse blocks.

Now, let's say that we have 8 x 4bar structures, roughly in story order that can form 2 or 3 verses and a chorus. Read through the whole set several times. What section stands out as the message or main theme of your song.

Identify one or two 4 bar sections that are the real essence of your song. 4 bars of lines work well for a snappy, concise type of message. If your message needs to say more, then 8 bars will usually accommodate it.

This structure will now form the chorus of your song. There's also a good chance that you can now extract the title of your song from the chorus, (if you don't already have one) as remember, the chorus is the central, main theme that your song is all about. In my own experience the song title has usually jumped out by now. Take some time now to form a song title, remember, nothing is set in stone, you can always change it later.

Select from your 4 and 8 bar sections the verses and chorus that you are going to use for your song. Write them down in the same way as the example song lyric. Are there any lyrical hooks that seem to stand out as being really catchy, if not, can you maybe change one or two key words to form a hook.

You may at this point have some new ideas, a new line or maybe some word changes to make it flow better. That's great, just write them down.

Now we really do have something to work with. Write out the complete song in it's verse and chorus structure, does it flow, does it rhyme. The answer is probably not all of it. At this point you should release the poet in you. Try to get some flow and rhyme working for each 4 bar section in the verse and chorus sections. You may need to change some words, so make use of your rhyming dictionary. You may even find that swapping lines around or even rewriting one or two does the trick. The objective here is to get the song to flow and rhyme.

Condensing sentences

Now that we have a collection of sentences that are loosely formed from the beginning to the end of the song story, we need to start thinking about condensing and joining the more meaningful sentences and discarding those that don't really fit, think of it as pruning the roses or weeding the lawn.

When you have a collection of lines that make up your 4 bar section, write them down separately, on their own and start polishing it. By this I mean go over it's meaning again, does it still say what you want it to. Read it out loud or sing it, does it rhyme well or could you maybe replace one or two words to improve the flow. Spend some time with your thesaurus and rhyming dictionary manipulating and rewriting these sentences.

Now is a good time to introduce a set of song

lyrics so that we can better understand and examine the main points being made in these important sections. Please refer to Appendix B and examine the songs: you will find examples of the types of rhyme that we have discussed and simple free form verse that just flows, expressing feelings and emotions.

Vocal melody

Now we need to create a vocal melody for both the verse and chorus, it doesn't matter which one you create first. Now is the time to turn on your portable recording device.

Think about the national anthem, whistle it, hum it and then sing it. You have just performed a song, albeit without musical accompaniment . This is what we are going to do now to create the vocal melody for your chorus. You have already put rhyme and flow into the lines, so just take that process one step further and start singing the lines. You will find that some lines, especially pairs of lines almost create their own tune or melody as you sing them. Experiment by singing the beginning words in the line higher in pitch or vice versa, the same goes for words in the middle. You may find a nice way of singing a particular line, but the words don't quite rhyme or flow any more. Simply change some of the words to get the flow back. This is another example of polishing and you should apply this technique to all of the sections in your song until you are satisfied with your work. Just experiment and you will soon come up with a melody that you like, just remember that you will probably need to vary this melody between the verse and chorus to give your song some variation, to stop it getting boring.

Now write down your song in full, in the new order and sing it through a couple of times. Remember that the chorus vocal melody will be the same each time that it is repeated. The verse should also retain the same vocal form for each individual verse in your song, some variation is of course allowed, it's down to you, but don't loose the repetitive features of the vocal melody, as the listener usually likes to learn the melody of the song quickly, and of course likes to repeatedly sing or hum those sections that he likes.

At this point you should be able to sing your song into your recorder the whole way through. Again, as we did when forming the story lines, you may want to let the song rest for a day or so and then go back to your recording.

Play your song and read the lyrics, by this time you should be really starting to get to know the melody of the song. Does it still sound as you want it to, or have you had some new thoughts about changing part of it. Experimentation here is the 'name of the game' and it's a fun part of sonwriting, so don't be in a hurry to finish your lyrics. Rewrite, reform and polish until you are happy and have a new and complete set of lyrics and melody.

You have now been through the polishing process and you should have your latest draft of lyrics written out, along with a complete vocal melody of the song.

We now need to consider adding some musical harmony to basically complete the song. As you will see in the next section, it may still be the case that a further session of polishing the lyrics or the vocal melody will be required to fit in with the musical harmony and accompaniment that you will create.

If you are about to embark on learning a musical

instrument, be it an acoustic or electric guitar, please turn to appendix A where I have given a few hints and tips about getting started and, good luck.

Please remember that you do not have to be a good musician at this stage in order to start creating a musical accompaniment. After a few sessions on either instrument, you will be able to play a few chords, not necessarily being fluent at changing between chords at this stage, but be able to play individual chords fairly cleanly. This will now allow you to hear the different sounds of the various chords and to start thinking about fitting the higher and lower sounding chords with your higher and lower sounding vocal melody. This process will make you want to change between two chord shapes so that you can hear if the chords fit your song, so it's a great way to help you to learn your instrument as well.

Musical keys and chords

The theory of musical keys can be quite complicated, but you only need to know a few simple rules about them in order to start using them for your songwriting.

What is a musical key

A musical key is a collection of musical chords that sound good when played together. They have a tonal centre that the listener always wants to be around, so when the notes move away from that centre, it's a relief to the listener when the music returns to its tonal centre. It's also a way that various tensions and other emotions can be added into a piece of music.

The chords of a specific musical key are formed from the seven notes that are collectively known as the musical scale. The seven notes that can be used in revolving order are:

A B C D E F G

The name of the musical scale and key will always be the same, the only important rule here is that the scale starts ands ends with the same note

Example

The scale of 'C Major' starts and ends with the note of ' C ' therefore:

C D E F G A B C

are the notes of the ' C Major ' scale in that order.

The musical key comprises chords from the scale and are always formed in the same basic way.

Example

The major and minor chords from the key of ' C Major ' are formed in the following way:

1 11 111 1V V V1 V11 V111

C D   E   F G   A   B   C

Nb. Roman numerals are used to donate the order of the notes.

The Major cords are 1, 1V and V

Therefore:

1 11 111 1V V V1 V11 V111

C D E   **F G** A   B   C

are the Major chords i.e., C, F and G

The Minor chords are

11, 111 and V1

Therefore:

1 11 111 1V V V1 V11 V111
C **D** **E**   F G **A** B   C

are the Minor chords i.e., Dm, Em and Am (the lower
case 'm' denoting minor).
This method of identifying the major and minor chords is
true for any key.

As you will soon find out from your own experience, the tonal quality and mood conveyed between major and minor chords is significant, and can have an overall effect on the mood of the song. Major chords tend to be happy and lively, where as minor chords are more sombre and serious. This will have a big influence on your choice of chords for your musical accompaniment, is your song bright and breezy, or is it maybe sad and serious. Again it's these points that you learn on your songwriting journey that make it such an enjoyable and engrossing activity.

Musical keys also have another important part to play for the songwriter. They allow the chords that you are using to be raised or lowered in pitch to accommodate singers with higher or lower vocal ranges. This process of changing the pitch is known as transposition.

Most electronic keyboards have a button that allows the pitch to be raised or lowered or have a simple key change function.

The guitar also has a simple solution to key change, the 'Capo'. The full name is Capodastra. The capo works by clamping itself across the fret board. As you move it down the fret board, you change the musical key of your chords, but retain the same finger positions, so you don't have to learn new and sometimes difficult chords.

If you are learning the guitar at this stage, you will find it easier to use the major chords from the key of A major i.e., A, D and E, for your first attempts at putting together some chords that can support your song. A set of chords used like this is known as a 'chord progression'. These chords are not only popular for guitar based accompaniment, they are also fairly easy to finger on the fret board.

Experiment with playing these chords at different tempos, using four beats to the bar.

Hint

The *Tempo* is the speed at which a piece of music is played: it's speed, pulse or rhythm.

The *Beat* is better described as the *Rhythmic Beat.* Tap your hand against your leg in a steady continuous and constant way; now count one, two, three, four in repetition and emphasise the fourth beat by making it louder. You should now hear a constant repetition of four beats to the bar. If you speed up or slow down, then you are changing the tempo of the four beats to the bar that you are tapping.

Try playing:

D	D	D	D
A	A	A	A
D	D	D	D
A	A	A	A
E	E	E	E
A	A	A	A
E	E	E	E
A	A	A	A

You can hear from this simple example a nice sounding harmony starting to emerge.

The 3 chord trick

You can play the three major chords together, in

just about any order from any musical key and they will always sound good together. So any combination of A, D and E are going to work in your songwriting. Incidentally, the minor chords also work well together.

Many of the great songs from the top bands and artists from the 1950's to the present day use only three basic chords.

If you are learning the keyboard, try the chords from the key of ' C major ' i.e., C, F and G. Many songs from the likes of Bob Dylan and Phil Collins are built solely around these three chords.

Example

G	G	G	G
F	F	F	F
G	G	G	G
F	F	F	F
C	C	C	C
F	F	F	F
C	C	C	C
F	F	F	F

The musical palette

We already have a collection of six chords from the key of ' C major ' that we know are compatible and are going to sound good together, these are:

C   F   G   major chords

Dm   Em Am   minor chords

Note here that the three chord trick does not cross over between the major and minor chords. The fact that all of these chords are from the same musical key means that they have a similarity of sound, but you will have to work out by experimenting with them to get a good sounding chord progression that mixes major and minor chords together. Again, this is one of those great things about songwriting, being able to fuse together a number of chords in your own way to get the sound that you want.

Now use the same technique as before to identify the major and minor chords in some other keys. We have already touched on the key of 'A major', so just to recap, here are the major and minor chords of 'A major':

1 11 111 1V V V1 V11 V111

A B   C   D   E   F   G   A

Major chords are 1, 1V and V   =   A, D and E

Minor chords are   11, 111 and V1   =   Bm, Cm and Fm

The trick here is to carry out this exercise as you are practicing playing your guitar, the two go hand in hand. I would suggest at this stage that you include all of the chords that you learn from the keys that you choose, and only omit chords that you really don't like the sound of, or are a bit too difficult to master playing at present. You can always add them to your palette later. For now, trust in your ears and trust in your judgement, you are the songwriter.

I personally started building my musical palette with the key of 'C major' as this is the middle ground, musically speaking, of keys. A selection of these chords are found in many of the popular hit songs of the last five or six decades.

It is also good practice to look at sheet music

books or on the internet of songs that you like the sound of and see what chords are being used. You will notice that some songs don't seem to follow the rules and have a strange mix of chords from several different keys. That's fine, as long as it works and sounds good.

Hint

The process of changing key within a song is called modulation. Some purists don't like it very much because you are going away from the tonal centre of the music, but I encourage you to experiment and if it sounds good to you, then just be different. Incidentally, the Beatles were heavy users of modulation in their songwriting, enough said.

To finish the subject of the musical palette, try to visualise it, and draw it out on paper as a painter's palette. Imagine an oval palette with the major and minor chords of 'C major' in the middle and use this as your reference point. Place chords with a higher pitch sound to the right, and those with a lower pitch sound to the left. Chords that are brighter in sound I place above and the more sombre sounding ones below. This can be really useful when you are looking for a higher sounding chord, say in part of a progression, just look at your musical palette and try a few chords from the area of interest. It is the forming of a musical palette, the sounds that you like, that will start to create, along with your lyrics a unique musical style, i.e., you as a songwriter, an artist in your own right.

Building the harmony

The harmony is built around the process that we have covered in the last few lessons. It's about choosing a number of chords that you like the sound of, and that suit the mood of your song. Experiment with the playing order and you will soon find that a particular order starts to emerge which you can play with and eventually form a good chord progression.

You will usually use two chord progressions, one that is repeated for the verse and one that is repeated for the chorus. This is needed so that you can add contrast between the verse and chorus, just as you did with the lyrics.

It's now time to choose which chord progression

to use for the verse, and which one for the chorus. Consider the mood that you are trying to give your song. Also consider trying to make an impact in the chorus. Often, the progression that contains the higher pitched chords make a good choice for the chorus because it has the effect of taking the song to a higher level of excitement and energy.

It's a matter now of personal experimentation. Sing your vocal melody and experiment with different ways of fitting the melody to the chord progression, or vice versa. You may still find that you are changing words, or lines or chords to get the song flowing to your liking. When this process is complete for both verse and chorus, we need to link the two together. If you have used some of the same chords in both progressions then often one will flow naturally into the other. Sometimes however, this automatic linking or flow does not happen: it probably has not happened naturally because of the order and mix of the chords that you have used.

Hint

Learn from this because it can be a good way of creating a contrast between the verse and chorus. Now it's time to introduce the musical bridge.

The musical bridge

A bridge is a part of the song that links one section to another. It can be used in many ways, for example to add some variation before the last chorus, but we will use it in this exercise as a means of linking, or joining a verse and chorus that does not have a natural flow. Again, forming a bridge is all about experimenting with chords and often the lyrics as well. As with songwriting in general, it gets easier with practice and the experience that you gain every time that you write one. A bridge is usually quite short, consisting of only two or four bars, any longer and you could argue that it is in fact another verse. If the bridge is to simply link musically two chord progressions then two bars is often enough. You may find however, that as you experiment with this, some other words or ideas come into your head and you end up adding a part to your song structure. That's fine and is to be encouraged. All of this experimentation and creativity is being moulded together by you in your own unique way, fantastic.

There are no set rules about writing a bridge, but here's some tip's that might help:

1. If it's a musical bridge that simply links two sections together, keep it short, say one or two bars.

2. Try to use chords from the same musical key as the verse and chorus are written in.

Song construction – a summary of the main steps

Here is a summary of the main steps taken in writing a song:

1. Define the storyline and subject matter
2. Get the story down on paper

   Create short one line sentences of the whole story

3. Form the storyline
4. Apply rhyme and flow

   Create 4 bar structures

5. Decide on the song structure

   How many verses and chorus repeats

6. Create the vocal melody

   Verse vocal melody

Chorus vocal melody

Bridge – if required

7. Create the musical accompaniment

8 Record a 'demo'

So there we are, congratulations, we have now arrived at the point where you have written your first song. For those of you who did not play a musical instrument before using this book and who decided to give it a try, you deserve another big pat on the back. Just stick with it and practice as often as you can.

What next

So where do we go from here, well, to round off this introduction to the world of songwriting you might find the following points useful:

Copyright protection
Recording a 'demo'
Performing and publishing

Copyright protection

Intellectual copyright is a complicated area of law and varies from country to country. Before you send your work to a record company or give the song to an artist to use, make sure that you can prove that it belongs to, and was created by you. The most practical and economical way of doing this is to place your demo CD and written draft of your song into a strong envelope that can be well sealed. Write the contents onto the outside of the envelope and seal it with additional transparent tape so that anyone could see if it had been opened or not. Send it by registered post to yourself. Once you have signed for it and have it back in your possession, do not open it, put it somewhere safe to keep. If there is any disagreement in the future about the original ownership, then you will be able to produce the earliest record of your song as evidence. A British court will accept this as proof of ownership but remember, do not open it. If you are going to send your work to other countries, including the USA, then you would be best advised to spend some time on the internet to research the current requirements for copyright protection in that country.

Recording a 'demo'

This section really deserves a book in its own right, but let me outline, in very simple terms the main options that you have, and how I prefer to record a 'demo' CD.

Recording studio

This option is out of reach for most songwriters due to the cost. If you want to perform the 'demo' yourself, it's not only expensive, but the recording studio along with an engineer and producer can be a very intimidating place to be. By its very nature as opposed to a live gig, the recording has to be as near perfect as possible so your vocals and instrument playing will come under intense scrutiny. If you do not want to perform yourself, then you can have a studio and session musicians perform and produce your song for you, but the cost will just keep on rising depending on your requirements.

Home studio/bedroom recording

By far the best and most enjoyable option for those both starting out and the experienced songwriter working on a low budget. Again it's all about how much money you want to spend, so I will outline the two main options that can get you started at a reasonable cost. Don't forget that second-hand equipment is much cheaper than new and is an option worth considering

The options we are going to look at are a computer based setup where the computer can still be used for other purposes, and a dedicated hardware setup where some of the equipment can't be used for anything else.

Computer setup

This setup can be achieved fairly cheaply, but can be very complicated to get all of the software and hardware running properly together. When you have achieved this, your next problem is to learn how the software works in order to record and edit your song. This was similar to my first recording setup. In practice I found myself spending more time keeping the computer and equipment running, and less time actually recording my songs. That's not to say that this type of setup will not work perfectly well for you because it will, it's just my personal experience.

Dedicated hardware setup

There are of course many options here, ranging from hundreds to many thousands of pounds, but this is my preferred starter setup. This setup can be purchased new from under £1000, cheaper if you buy second-hand and has all of the facilities that you need to produce a professional sounding 'CD'. The heart of the system is a BOSS-BR900 8track digital recording studio. This unit has a built in drum machine and allows me to effortlessly record synch, guitar and vocals. It has an onboard guitar effects processor, a complete mastering facility and a built in CD writer.

Like any new equipment of this nature, you will need to spend some time learning how to use it, but I didn't find it too complicated. The downside to this setup is that you can't use it for anything else, except playing CD's.

Performing and publishing

Now that you have some songs and a 'demo CD', what are you going to do with them. The choice of course is totally yours. You may be content to just play your CD to yourself and simply practice songwriting as a hobby. A very pleasant pastime, but I would suggest that you at least get a few friends to listen to your work so that you can get some real feedback. Critique or honest criticism can only help you develop as a songwriter. You don't have to agree with it, but it will at least make you consider your work from another perspective. Just be aware that close friends and relatives might not give you a totally honest opinion for fear of offending your feelings.

You could also place a newspaper advertisement, seeking a co-writer to collaborate with, or you could approach a local band or artist to ask if they would like to use some of your work. If you perform local gigs yourself, then you are going to get lots of feedback and you may even start building a local fan base.

If you are really seeking fame and fortune then you need to start approaching the professional side of the music industry. Send your 'demo' CD of only two or three tracks directly to producers and agents, but be aware that you may not get it back as these people are listening to many artists every day. If you feel that your style of song is particularly suited to a certain artist then some research on the internet will usually find a contact point through an agent or record company where you can send your 'demo', but always ask first, that way you have a much better chance of having your CD listened to. Record companies have an A&R department (artists & repertoire), contact them by email and ask how you can submit a demo. You may be able to email an MP3 file to them which is a fairly straight forward process.

Finally, I should mention the internet, as this is fast becoming the place to be heard and to get feedback. There are many websites that allow you to upload your profile and songs for others to listen to. It's also becoming common place for record companies and agents to scan these sites looking for new artists and indeed, many artists that make it commercially are now discovered on these internet sites. If you do choose to use a website, be sure to check on the terms and conditions of the site and make sure that you retain the copyright to your song and any other material after you have uploaded it. As you can now see, there are many options available to you and as always, the choice is yours. You may remember that I said in the introduction that songwriting will open many new doors for you, well, if you have come this far then I am sure that you would now agree.

Thank you for coming on this journey with me, and I sincerely hope that you have now emerged as a new artist and songwriter and will go on to greater things. Any feedback or comments are always welcomed on graham@verseology.co.uk or visit the web site at www.verseology.co.uk

Appendix A

Getting started on Guitar

Your first Guitar

This getting started section is suitable for any type of guitar that you choose to start with e.g., Acoustic, Semi Acoustic or Electric.

The ease of use of an Acoustic guitar where no amplifiers or other electronic equipment needs to be plugged in or connected, certainly makes it the preferred choice for me. Another important point is that you get a true tone from the instrument, so you can hear the subtle differences between closely related chords. This can be lost when using amplified instruments that use some degree of distortion or overdrive to gain other effects.

Acoustic guitars can be loosely divided into two groups, those that use Nylon strings and those that use Steel strings. There is a distinct, if somewhat subtle difference in their sound with the Nylon strings offering a richer tone that tends to suit folk songs and the like, whilst the Steel strings are very well suited to rhythm sections in modern pop songs. This is of course a subjective view, but it should give you an idea of the type of differences that may influence your choice of instrument.

Hint

Nylon strung guitars replicate the traditional Spanish classical guitar and have a wider neck/fret board. If you are just starting out and you have larger hands and fingers, then you may find it easier to finger chords cleanly with this type of guitar.

Again, this point demonstrates the many subtle differences that may influence your choice of guitar. I would strongly suggest that you hold and try the different types at your local shop. Not only are the staff usually knowledgeable, I have always found them more than willing to let you try out the various choices. Don't be afraid to tell them that you are just starting to learn to play the instrument, you will get better suited advice, and maybe even a free lesson.

Another opinion that I must point out here is about the cost of your first guitar. I would suggest that you purchase a reasonable priced factory made guitar, Yamaha and Fender spring to mind. Avoid expensive hand made guitars until you really know what suits you best. The factory 'production line' guitars still sound good and are more likely to have correctly sounding notes up and down the fret board, where the cheaper range of 'hand made' can sometimes be flawed.

Getting started

The first step in getting started is to buy yourself an electronic tuner. These devices are cheap to buy, and some even show you the finger positions for hundreds of chords. There is nothing worse and demoralising than trying to play your first chords, and they just sound terrible, and they will sound terrible if the guitar is out of tune. So it is essential that you get into the habit of tuning your guitar every time that you pick it up to play.

Hint

New strings take a little time to settle down, so expect to

make quite a few adjustments, especially if you are using nylon strings. Nylon strings can take several days to stretch and become consistent in holding a note.

Tuning the guitar

The standard tuning is:

Low
 E A D G B E
The low E string is the thickest string at the top of the guitar as you play.

Take your time and get the tuning right. When your guitar is in tune, finger the individual strings slowly from top to bottom and get to learn the sounds. Don't worry at this point in time with other tunings that you may have heard about, stick with the standard tunings for now, there will be plenty of time in the future for experimenting with alternative tunings.

As I have already suggested in the main text, start off with the major chords from the key of A major i.e., A Major, D Major and E Major, (usually denoted as simply A, D and E using capital letters and dropping the word major).

Play each chord on its own with a gentle down stroke, followed by an up stroke. At first you will produce a buzzing sound from some strings and a dull, dampened sound from others. This will happen when your finger is not pressing down cleanly on the string, or is touching an adjacent string that it shouldn't be. Practice is the only way forward here, but you will quickly learn how to play the chord cleanly, i.e., crisp clear notes with no buzzes.

The next object of this exercise is to put together a simple, but good sounding chord progression using just three chords. This will allow you to create some musical accompaniment for a verse or chorus.

Refer back to the *3 chord trick* section as necessary, but listen to how these three major chords from the key of A Major sound good in just about any order. Experiment with using different plectrums to strum both up and down strokes. Try using your finger nails or your thumb to sound all or just some of the strings. When you add these different techniques to variations in tempo or beats to the bar, you will realise just how many different musical sounds and variations can be made by just using three chords.

Practice and patience is now what it is all about: you will find that the skin on your finger tips begin to develop a hard pad, so it becomes less painful to finger the strings; but more importantly you will find that your fingers, as if by some sort of magic, seems to automatically place themselves onto the frets in the correct positions, without you even having to look, incredible!

When you have reached the stage where you can change your finger positions cleanly and rhythmically through these three chords, the world is your oyster!

I suggest that you now refer back to the section on the *musical palette*, and start creating a musical palette of your own. The major and minor chords from the key of C major, that we have looked at together, combine well with what you have learnt so far, 'bon voyage' and good luck.

Appendix B

*The song title – **Beyond Love***

This is one of my early songs and I can still vividly remember writing it. There was so much emotion and love that had built up inside of me, when I put myself into the focus zone and started to concentrate on writing the lyrics, words and sentences came flowing out of my mind faster that I could write them down on paper. That in itself was quite an experience because at the end of it I felt quite relieved in a strange sort of way, as though I had been wanting to say these things for a long time but had never found the right time or place to say them.

The background to the song

This song tells of love and an emotional attachment between two people, two souls, that goes beyond our normal understanding of unrelenting love to a place somewhere in the ether, the unknown. This feeling or sense isn't documented because there is no physical evidence to support it, but I know it exists because I feel it, but can't explain it. It's similar to the spirit world where there is no real scientific evidence to support it, but if you have ever had a paranormal experience then you know that there's something there, you just can't explain it.

In this song the emotional attachment is between myself and my son. He was born by caesarean section and handed to me, just after his birth, wrapped simply in a towel. As a first time father I wasn't sure what he was going to look like, or even if I would be able to recognize him. It was to my utter amazement that not only could I recognize him, I could have picked him out of a line of a hundred babies. It took only a second or so before our eyes met and it's a moment in my life that I still can't explain, but when I looked into his eyes there was an intensity that I could feel, but not explain. It only lasted for a couple of seconds, but for me will remain in my memory forever as a very powerful emotional attachment that can't physically be explained. I believe that this moment of mystery will stay with my spirit, my soul, forever, and will travel to wherever destiny takes it in the future.

Beyond Love

The first time our senses met

That first glance into his eyes

A moment of mystery

Joining our souls magically

Forces known only by the gods

Beyond life's comprehension

A bond thicker than blood

That transcends eternity

Oh the miracle of life (chorus)

The chemistry between two souls

Something beyond love

Something that lasts past life's end

All our lifetime through (verse 2)

That love and understanding

Through the bad times to

When our lives fell apart

But we overcame those times

to grow stronger together

We found a new way of life

When ever we shared time together

Oh the miracle of life   (chorus)

The chemistry between two souls

Something beyond love

Something that lasts past life's end

Now our lives go separate way's (verse 3)

And we live far apart

But the bond is always there

Growing stronger every day

And when we meet from time to time

Words aren't even needed

Just one glance into his eye's

And everything is said

Oh the miracle of life (chorus)

The chemistry between two soul

Something beyond love

Something that lasts past life's end

One option here would have been to modify the final
chorus so that we could round the song off with a slightly
different ending. Another would be to omit the final
chorus and just finish the song on verse three.

The song title – *Love, Guilt & Hate*

This song sadly, is about relationships breaking up; it happens all too often in the modern world and affects most of us, sometime in our lifetime. Animosity is often felt by one of the couple who are breaking up, leaving a feeling of love, guilt & hate.

<u>Love, Guilt & Hate</u>

I still remember, the day you first left
Like a video playing, inside my head
why couldn't you tell me that something was wrong
To let me understand, and take things on
You just upped and walked away, out of my life Leaving
me sad and lonely, not knowing what was right
What was it that I did, to deserve this fate   That fills me
with torment, love guilt and hate

Every day I ask why this happened to me *chorus*
Is this really, my destiny
Will I ever love again that smile of my dreams
That brings joy and happiness to the heart of me

Can I ever trust again, deep in my heart
To set my soul free, and make a new start

Now that you're gone, the hurt lingers on
As I sit and ponder, how my life can move on
Will I feel this hatred, for the rest of my life
Or will my senses harden, and turn guilt into strife
Was this really destiny, showing me the way
Or one of past life's forces, having their day
What was it that I did, to deserve this fate
That fills me with torment, love guilt and hate

Every day I ask why this happened to me
Is this really, my destiny
Will I ever love again that smile of my dreams
That brings joy and happiness to the heart of me
Can I ever trust again, deep in my heart
To set my soul free, and make a new start

The song title – *When Spirits Intertwine*

A true love song from a real experience, maybe one day
I'll send her a copy?

When Spirits Intertwine

She's danced in my head, for week upon week
That sweet sweet smile, so gentle and meek
The picture of beauty, that turned my head
Now fills my heart, with yearning
With you is where, I have to be
Some day in the future, for all to see
Oh my Sarah, I love you so
Just let our spirits embrace, and glow

Let me touch with you, let me be with you
Let me sense your sweet perfume
Let me hold you in my arms, your body close to mine
Let me feel the sensations, when spirits intertwine
When spirits intertwine

Bring me happiness, and show me joy

Help me to say goodbye

To the loneliness that lives deep within

Without you I think I'll just die

Give me your heart, and your soul will follow

Come join with me, for all of tomorrow

Join me and learn, what life can be like

In true love, and senses that delight

Let me touch with you, let me be with you

Let me sense your sweet perfume

Let me hold you in my arms, your body close to mine

Let me feel the sensations, when spirits intertwine

When spirits intertwine